THE ENCYCLOPEDIA OF PSYCHOACTIVE DRUGS

IN 25 VOLUMES
Each title on a specific drug or drug-related problem

ESCAPE FROM ANXIETY & STRESS

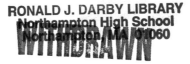

THE ENCYCLOPEDIA OF PSYCHOACTIVE DRUGS

ESCAPE FROM ANXIETY & STRESS

TOM McLELLAN, Ph.D.

University of Pennsylvania

GENERAL EDITOR (U.S.A)
Professor Solomon H. Snyder, M.D.

*Distinguished Service Professor of
Neuroscience, Pharmacology, and Psychiatry at
The Johns Hopkins University School of Medicine*

SE 6 '97

GENERAL EDITOR (U.K.)
Professor Malcolm H. Lader, D.Sc.,Ph.D.,F.R.C.Psych.

*Professor of Clinical Psychopharmacology
at the Institute of Psychiatry, University of London,
and Honorary Consultant to the Bethlem Royal and Maudsley Hospitals*

Burke Publishing Company Limited

LONDON   TORONTO   NEW YORK

Acknowledgements
Photos courtesy of AP/World Wide Photos, Art Resource, BBC Hulton Picture
Library, New Line Cinema, The Photo Co-op Library, St Bartholomew's Hospital,
Science Photo Library, UPI/Bettmann Newsphotos.

CIP data
McLellan, Tom
    Escape from anxiety and stress (Encyclopedia of psychoactive drugs)
    1. Alcoholism and drug abuse. Role of stress
    I. Title. II Series.
    616.86'071
    ISBN 0 222 01463 6 Hardbound
    ISBN 0 222 01464 4 Paperback

Burke Publishing Company Limited
Pegasus House, 116-120 Golden Lane, London EC1Y 0TL, England
Printed in Spain, by Jerez Industrial, S.A.

CONTENTS

Stress affects people of all ages. It can be debilitating and cause anxiety, depression, and physical symptoms such as a dry mouth and upset stomach, or be positive and stimulate the desire to achieve, in which case it is called "eustress", without which few things would be accomplished.

INTRODUCTION

*T*he late twentieth century has seen the rapid growth of both the legitimate medical use and the illicit, non-medical abuse of an increasing number of drugs which affect the mind. Both use and abuse are very high in general in the United States of America and great concern is voiced there. Other Western countries are not far behind and cannot afford to ignore the matter or to shrug off the consequent problems. Nevertheless, differences between countries may be marked and significant: they reflect such factors as social habits, economic status, attitude towards the young and towards drugs, and the ways in which health care is provided and laws are enacted and enforced.

Drug abuse particularly concerns the young but other age groups are not immune. Alcoholism in middle-aged men and increasingly in middle-aged women is one example, tranquillizers in women another. Even the old may become alcoholic or dependent on their barbiturates. And the most widespread form of addiction, and the one with the most dire consequences to health, is cigarette-smoking.

Why do so many drug problems start in the teenage and even pre-teenage years? These years are critical in the human life-cycle as they involve maturation from child to adult. During these relatively few years, adolescents face the difficult task of equipping themselves physically and intellectually for adulthood and of establishing goals that make adult life worthwhile while coping with the search for personal identity, assuming their sexual roles and learning to come to terms with authority. During this intense period of growth and activity, bewilderment and conflict are inevitable, and peer pressure to experiment and to escape from life's apparent problems becomes overwhelming. Drugs are increasingly available and offer a tempting respite.

Unfortunately, the consequences may be serious. But the penalties for drug-taking must be put into perspective. Thus, addicts die from heroin addiction but people also die from alcoholism and even more from smoking-related diseases. Also, one must separate the direct effects of drug-taking from those indirectly related to the life-style of so many addicts. The problems of most addicts include many factors other than drug-taking itself. The chaotic existence or social deterioration of some may be the cause rather than the effect of drug abuse.

Drug use and abuse must be set into its social context. It reflects a complex interaction between the drug substance (naturally-occurring or synthetic), the person (psychologically normal or abnormal), and society (vigorous or sick). Fads affect drug-taking, as with most other human activities, with drugs being heavily abused one year and unfashionable the next. Such swings also typify society's response to drug abuse. Opiates were readily available in European pharmacies in the last century but are stringently controlled now. Marijuana is accepted and alcohol forbidden in many Islamic countries; the reverse obtains in most Western countries.

The use of psychoactive drugs dates back to prehistory. Opium was used in Ancient Egypt to alleviate pain and its main constituent, morphine, remains a favoured drug for pain relief. Alcohol was incorporated into religious ceremonies in the cradles of civilization in the Near and Middle East and has been a focus of social activity ever since. Coca leaf has been chewed by the Andean Indians to lessen fatigue; and its modern derivative, cocaine, was used as a local anaesthetic. More recently, a succession of psychoactive drugs have been synthesized, developed and introduced into medicine to allay psychological distress and to treat psychiatric illness. But, even so, these innovations may present unexpected problems, such as the difficulties in stopping the long-term use of tranquillizers or slimming-pills, even when taken under medical supervision.

The Encyclopedia of Psychoactive Drugs provides information about the nature of the effects on mind and body of alcohol and drugs and the possible results of abuse. Topics include where the drugs come from, how they are made, how they affect the body and how the body deals with these

In the late 1800s Vin Mariani was widely consumed in Europe and the United States. Described in this poster as a "French tonic wine" that "restores health and vitality", Vin Mariani contained cocaine.

Thomas Edison, the inventor of the phonograph and the light bulb, was, along with such celebrities as the author Jules Verne, one of many people who endorsed cocaine-containing Vin Mariani at the turn of the century.

chemicals; the effects on the mind, thinking, emotions, the will and the intellect are detailed; the processes of use and abuse are discussed, as are the consequences for everyday activities such as school work, employment, driving, and dealing with other people. Pointers to identifying drug users and to ways of helping them are provided. In particular, this series aims to dispel myths about drug-taking and to present the facts as objectively as possible without all the emotional distortion and obscurity which surrounds the subject. We seek neither to exaggerate nor to play down the complex topics concerning various forms of drug abuse. We hope that young people will find answers to their questions and that others — parents and teachers, for example — will also find the series helpful.

The series was originally written for American readers by American experts. Often the problem with a drug is particularly pressing in the USA or even largely confined to that country. We have invited a series of British experts to adapt the series for use in non-American English-speaking countries and believe that this widening of scope has successfully increased the relevance of these books to take account of the international drug scene.

This volume deals with one of the background areas to drug dependence. Some individuals seem to develop drug or alcohol problems because they find these substances lessen their levels of anxiety and thereby help them to cope with stresses in their lives. Later, this becomes a reliance on the substances and eventually dependence and abuse problems develop.

Written by Tom McLellan, Alicia Bragg and John Cacciola and adapted by Malcolm Bruce, this book outlines the topics of stress and anxiety and reviews the effects of various drugs, licit and illicit, on the symptoms of anxiety.

M. H. Lader

The film Reefer Madness is an example of the ineffectiveness of scare tactics. Produced in the 1930s to discourage marijuana use, the film exaggerated the drug's hazards, and is now viewed as a comedy.

AUTHOR'S PREFACE

People most commonly use drugs or alcohol for recreational purposes because these substances are reputed to increase enjoyment or reduce the unpleasantness of a boring, lonesome, anxious, or otherwise stressful situation. In an effort to discourage recreational drug use, scare tactics emphasizing negative effects have frequently been used. Nevertheless, the simple facts are that most of the available drugs (including alcohol) do have very powerful effects on mood and under certain conditions can enhance the pleasure of good times and alleviate the discomfort of bad times.

This book was written not to scare, but to explore, honestly and intelligently, the facts about drug usage and stress — how drugs work, their immediate effects on the body, and their overall impact on the individual and society.

Specifically, three types of commonly available drugs — alcohol, marijuana, and the stimulants — will be examined, focusing on their effects, the biological and situational factors that influence the nature of these effects, and the reason these drugs make a person feel good, especially during periods of stress.

In order to better understand drugs and stress one must first understand the common emotional problems that often accompany stress and the nature of stress and its effects, both positive and negative, on the body, the mind, and particularly on the emotional state, or "mood". These subjects will be discussed, particularly stressing the importance of developing strategies for dealing with these effects.

Finally, the book looks at the effectiveness of drugs as stress-relievers. Data accumulated from ten years of research have shown that people who use available street drugs to "handle" or "get through" problems of anxiety, depression, loneliness, and boredom do indeed get some benefits from these drugs. However, these people also run the risk of developing a drug habit and chronic emotional problems, often the problems they originally used the drugs to avoid.

The facts presented here should make it possible for an individual to make an informed choice regarding the best strategy for handling the stress that is an unavoidable part of everyday life.

Stress is often a contributor to heart failure, the leading cause of death in the Western world. This computer, which simulates cardiac arrest, trains medical students to respond swiftly and accurately.

CHAPTER 1

STRESS AND ITS CONSEQUENCES

*I*n our high-pressure, high-tech society, stress has become an everyday word. It is the topic of television talk shows and the primary focus of several kinds of psychotherapy. Stress-management workshops are popular on college campuses and among high-powered business executives. Throughout the nation, people young and old are seeking new strategies to cope with stress.

What Is Stress?

According to Dr Hans Selye, a leading authority on the subject, stress is simply the "nonspecific response of the body to any demand". Stress is always present, accompanying every human activity, whether it be physical, intellectual, emotional, or social. The only time we are really free from stress is when we are dead.

In most cases the word "stress" conjures up a negative image. This is because stress is generally associated with "distress", a condition which ranges from being mildly unpleasant to extremely dangerous, causing such physical illnesses as headache, ulcers, and even heart disease.

All stress is not bad, however. Not only can it be positive but it can actually be curative. This type of stress, known as "eustress", serves as a stimulus to action, and without it little would get done in the world.

Stress Affects Everyone Differently

How people react to stress varies greatly. A situation that evokes a high level of stress in one person may barely elicit a response from another person.

An illustrative example is one's first dive from the high diving board. Recall how it felt to climb the ladder, step to the board's edge, leap into the air, and plunge into the water. The experience may have been exhilarating or terrifying, depending on who you are or perhaps even on what day it occurred. For one person it may be the inspiration for an Olympic diving career. For another person it may inspire only a fervent "never again". The act of diving is consistent, but for one the resulting stress is positive, a spur to accomplishment. For the other, the stress is excessive and negative, and becomes a deterrent to action.

The Many Forms of Stress

Whenever a physical or emotional demand is made of the body, it experiences stress. Any type of demand may cause either a physical and/or an emotional response. A physical response may include perspiration, the shakes, or even exhaustion.

Stress is most commonly perceived as an emotional response, however. Generally, one associates stress only with

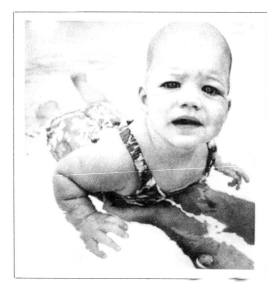

The babies pictured on this and the following page illustrate two types of responses to a new and potentially threatening situation — the first swimming lesson. This 7-month-old baby responded by displaying anxiety and apprehension.

negative emotional responses, such as anxiety, tension, or depression, but positive emotional reactions, such as excitement or exhilaration, are also responses to certain types of stressful situations. Within the broad framework, most, if not all, emotions are stress reactions — that is, responses to the demands of everyday life.

Problems Demand Solutions

Situations that require solutions and thus create stress occur in all areas and at all times of life. In every one of the following examples, the individual experiences stress, though it may be perceived and acted upon in various ways:

a) One-year-old Jane wants to move from the hallway to the door;

b) Ten-year-old Bob discovers that the kid up the street took his bike after his parents told him never to let anyone ride it;

c) Sixteen-year-old Mary has two minutes to solve a difficult word problem on a maths exam before the bell rings.

In analyzing situations such as these, one tends to put them into categories. Jane's problem is physical; Bob's is emotional; and Mary's is intellectual. However, the process that each of these individuals uses to solve his or her problem

Unlike the baby shown on the previous page, this 10-month-old infant seems relaxed and, indeed, truly delighted by his first experience in a swimming pool.

does, in fact, involve a combination of thought, emotion, and action.

It is easy to see that Jane's problem — that of getting from the hallway to the door — requires a physical response. Less obvious, however, is the intellectual response that must occur before any movement is possible. For mature individuals, the thought processes involved in moving from one place to another are so automatic that they occur without our being conscious of them. For a baby, however, the solution to the problem of locomotion is more complex. The infant may have to decide whether to crawl or to walk — an intellectual response. Furthermore, a baby is exhilarated by moving from hallway to door — an emotional response. And only after these responses does the infant actually move — a physical response.

The combined intellectual-emotional demands of the third type of problem are probably easier to recognize: "If a farmer picked one and one-half bushels of apples in three hours, how many bushels of apples . . . ?" Confronted with such a problem and given a limited amount of time in which to respond, different students will have different emotional stress responses. One may experience dread: "Oh, no! I hate word problems! I never get them right!" While another will

Infants line up for a baby-crawling contest. The ensuing race served as an early introduction to the stressful nature of competition, a facet of life that causes anxiety for people of all ages. The contest forced the babies to respond physically, emotionally, and even intellectually, for coupled with the exhilaration of competing was the struggle of deciding how to reach the finish line.

respond with: "Oh, I love word problems! They're so much fun!"

These emotional states may also be accompanied by a physical response. Dread often causes a queasy stomach, a dry mouth, or shortness of breath. Emotional excitement, on the other hand, is often characterized by deeper breathing, increased energy, or perhaps a fluttering stomach. Of course, the emotional and physical responses will also be partially governed by the student's intellectual ability to handle the problem, or even his or her perception of this ability.

The borrowed-bicycle problem is probably first experienced as an emotional one. Nevertheless, a good deal of intellectual and even physical effort may be necessary to solve the problem. The level of stress involved will depend upon the circumstances. If the friend who took the bicycle was unaware of the parents' rule, the solution might be a simple appeal to friendship and reason: "I'm sorry, but my parents told me not to let anyone ride it. Please give me back by bike". Some degree of mental and emotional discomfort is experienced, but it is probably minimal. If, on the other hand, the bike was taken with full knowledge of the rule and by the neighbourhood bully, the level of stress will undoubtedly be great. The immediate response is emotional: fear, or maybe anger. Then follows the intellectual response: "How do I get the bike back?" Finally, there may be a tough physical response: Grab the bike and run!

In the discussion of these problems, it is important to realize that each of the three aspects of our personality —

An eight-year-old boy learns computer programming in a classroom. The widespread publicity regarding the necessity to own and understand computers has produced tension and anxiety in school administrators, educators, parents, and their children.

intellectual, emotional, and physical — operates independently. They are delicately woven together to make up the human fabric.

Awareness of this interdependence is necessary when analyzing a problem. A situation that initially seems to evoke only an emotional response upon closer consideration will most likely reveal a physical element as well. For example, a condition of emotional stress, such as anxiety or depression, is almost always accompanied by a physical response, such as sleeplessness, loss of appetite, headache, and upset stomach.

Fine-Tuning Our Personality

Most likely, at some point in everyone's life a teacher has suggested that a good night's sleep and a good breakfast would help improve the quality of one's school work. This advice reflected the teacher's awareness of the relatedness of physical health to not only intellectual performance, but to emotional and social adjustment.

As a person passes from infancy into childhood, from childhood into adolescence, and from adolescence into adulthood, he or she encounters new and ever more difficult

Physical activity such as bike riding is an effective way to relieve daily tension.

problems. Human development is not a simple task. Change and growth are a lifelong process. As one matures, he or she becomes increasingly able to control this change and growth and, consequently, the responsibility for the development becomes increasingly one's own. This development takes place in the physical, intellectual, emotional, and social realms.

Because of the importance and interdependency of these realms there is the need to keep all the parts of the mind and body well balanced and in good working order, just as one would the parts of an automobile engine. A person must always strive to learn more, exercise as much as possible, study, sleep, and always try to get along with and respect other people.

This requires a lot of work, frequently too much. The mind and body work together to regulate how well a person takes care of him- or herself, and usually provide warning signals when the stress is too great. The response to excessive physical, intellectual, and/or emotional stimulation may be fatigue. Both the body and mind require time to adjust and adapt. Too many stress-producing situations can result in physical or emotional illness.

Millions of Chinese daily practice tai chi chuan, *an ancient martial art that is both rigorous and relaxing.*

Body image is so important that many people spend hours trying to attain perfection. Yoga has the additional bonus that, if practised 'mindfully', it not only aids the physical body but also relieves tension and stress.

CHAPTER 2

MAJOR CAUSES OF STRESS

Stressors, or the conditions that produce stress, generally fall into four categories: physical appearance and well-being; social situations and interpersonal relationships; school or job; and the family. Asked to analyze one's life, one would most likely be able to place his or her problems into one or more of these categories. The specific details may vary from person to person, but the general themes remain the same.

Physical Appearance and Well-Being

Throughout most people's lives, body image is a major concern. No matter what, one tends to perceive his or her body as imperfect. There is either too much here, not enough there, too little everywhere, or more than enough all over!

Adolescents are particularly sensitive about their physical appearance. This sensitivity concerning body image is part of the search for identity that characterizes adolescence. In addition, during this period increased production of hormones in the body causes many physical changes, such as the development of breasts and the growth of facial and genital hair. Appearance may reflect a desire to belong, to be like everyone else. Or, conversely, one's appearance may be used to express individuality or independence. No matter how a person chooses to appear — to him- or herself, to peers, or to adults — every decision regarding this image may cause stress.

Social Situations and Interpersonal Relationships

The development of sexual interest greatly contributes to adolescent stress. During this time dating begins, and the word "relationship" takes on a new meaning. Although one tries to be "cool", this new intimacy, while important, is also threatening.

Suddenly friendship takes on special significance, and the peer group becomes particularly powerful in determining what is acceptable and what is not acceptable. For most young people, having friends is crucial, and not having them can be a source of great unhappiness. In fact, to some adolescents, popularity is a measure of a person's value. The opinion and esteem of one's friends begins to carry as much, if not more, weight as those of one's parents. This can sometimes lead to open conflict at home. More often, however, the result is an internal struggle as one is faced with the problem of having to choose between what one wants to do and what one feels he or she is supposed to do.

Because of these pressures, social situations that are supposed to be fun — parties, dances, athletic events — can become a continuous stream of challenges related to one theme: social acceptance or rejection. "I wonder if she likes me?" "I wonder if *he* likes me?" "Should I ask her out?" "Should *I* ask *him* out?" "Will he notice me?" "What'll I do if no one talks to me?" "What if someone *does* talk to me?"

Nearly everyone eventually faces at least one of these questions. Whether one is relaxed or tense, popular or unpopular, social situations are stressful for nearly everyone. Part of growing up is learning to develop the skills to deal with this stress so that any social situation can be enjoyable.

School and Job

Two environments that are central to one's life and thus are major causes of stress are one's school and job. Because contemporary society emphasizes the importance of these areas, one's success or failure in them is often seen as a measure of a person's self-worth.

The school system, like society at large, rewards success, and penalizes, or at best ignores, failure. This highly competitive system is stressful for everyone, achiever and nonachiever alike. When a teacher uses the school prize winner as a role model, less successful students may feel so

26

over-whelmed by their own lesser achievements that they are too discouraged to attempt to compete at all. In response to this stress, the student drops out, either physically and/or mentally.

The school prize winner's response to the competition is less readily apparent, but nonetheless real. The overachiever must deal with taunts such as "teacher's pet" and "egghead", or the barbed (and secretly envious) comment, "I suppose you got another 'A' ". Perhaps worst of all, overachievers feel that they can never let up for a minute, that no matter what the cost they must maintain the same high level of achievement, and that they must fulfil other people's expectations rather than their own.

The same type of competition continues in the work world. In most workplaces employees take note of who works hardest and who "skives off", who deserves and gets

Two pupils help each other solve a maths problem in school. In non Cosmopolitan areas, initial inter-racial mixing of children can cause tension and anxiety, especially among parents.

rewards, and who gets rewards but does not deserve them. However, competition, like social relations, cannot — and should not — be avoided. Rather, here too a person must develop strategies and skills to handle the stress. This might mean channelling the stress into a search for a better understanding of the whole situation, or it might include learning how to analyze a particular situation in order to determine how it could be changed to benefit everyone. The "distress" must be turned into "eustress" — stress must work for, rather than against, us.

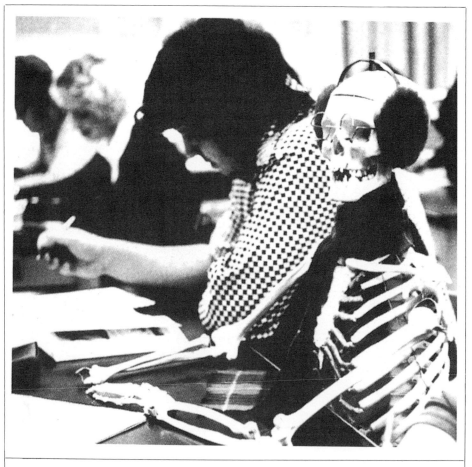

"Really boning up for the exam": To ease the tension during a biology test, the creative teacher placed this skeleton at a desk.

Family Relationships

A person's relations with his or her family is particularly stressful during adolescence. Even the happiest and most secure home has an occasional conflict. The dispute might be over something as seemingly unimportant as taking out the rubbish. Sometimes, as adolescents try to assert their independence, the conflict is more serious. A seemingly innocuous question such as "When are you going to get your hair cut?" can be interpreted as a parental threat and an unfair interference in one's lifestyle. Often, parents are simply unaware, or unwilling to admit, that their child is growing

Perhaps slightly exaggerated in its comic depiction of man versus machine, the Charlie Chaplin film classic Modern Times *nevertheless makes an accurate statement of just how stressful our fast-paced society can be.*

up and is now better able to take care of him- or herself.

Another common source of family friction is sibling rivalry. While they jockey for first place in parents' hearts, children often reveal the stress they are experiencing through such remarks as: "Mum always did like you best". "How come he got more cake than I did?" "Why do I always get the hand-me-downs?" This competition often spills over into other areas of life. At school, for instance, the maths teacher's innocent remark at roll call on the first day of class, "Mary Webster, Allison's sister? I only hope you will be the same kind of model pupil she was", only serves to intensify the competition.

A portrait, taken in the 1800s, of four generations of a single family. Until about 50 years ago, it was usual for all family members to live near each other, thus ensuring mutual emotional support. Today's shrinking family provides much less support during times of stress.

Of course, a family is much more than just a context for confrontations between family members. Even in families where the competition is the hottest, when the honour or safety of any member is challenged by an outsider, the family usually closes ranks. "I can fight with my sister, I can call her every name in the book, but don't let anyone else dare put her down, or they'll have to deal with me!"

Because the family is so important and the relationships within it are so closely intertwined, when a breakdown of the family unit occurs it is extremely stressful. The emotions brought out by such an event generally outweigh anything connected with sibling rivalries or clashes between parents

Franz Kafka (1883-1924), the Czech author of such fiction as The Trial *and* The Castle. *Kafka's writings, reflecting his own struggle with his frequently violent, unsympathetic father as well as with the world around him, often dealt with the stressful nature of family relationships and the individual's attempt to survive in modern society.*

and children. Marital separation or divorce, although sometimes necessary for the ultimate well-being of all family members, can have an immediate and a long-term distressing effect on everyone involved. Over time, family members usually learn to cope better with the stress of this major alteration in their lives, and over time the emotional upheaval subsides to some extent. However, during the initial period of adjustment, everyone involved is more vulnerable to the negative effects of everyday stress.

The most stressful situation for a family is the serious illness or death of a family member. To experience different emotions — anger, fear, guilt, sadness — is common during such times. Sometimes one imagines he or she is somehow

The parents of these children, who are in the crèche of a court building, are involved in divorce proceedings. Children often wrongly blame themselves for the problems of their parents.

responsible for the sickness that has befallen the other person. Or there is fear of being left behind, or anger at being abandoned. ''What will I do without him?.'' ''How could she go away and leave me all alone?'' When a close family member dies, the stress is enormous. However, the passage of time and the process of grieving — talking about the loss, sharing feelings, recalling past memories — allow a person gradually to adjust to even this most stressful of events.

To explore the stresses of marriage and parenthood, these American sociology students pretended that they were married and that the egg in the basket was their child.

The Henry Moore sculpture Family Group *(1945 – 1949) illustrates the importance of the family to each of its members, especially the infant, who depends physically and emotionally on his or her parents.*

CHAPTER 3

EARLY EMOTIONAL AND SOCIAL DEVELOPMENT

How one copes with stress depends on many factors. One of the most important is a person's childhood experiences. An infant's survival is entirely dependent upon the people who take care of it, and their importance to the infant's emotional and social growth cannot be overestimated.

From the moment the infant is held it begins to develop a strong emotional bond with its parents. The quality of this bond strongly affects a person's development, for throughout life it influences the way he or she will interact with the world.

The quality of the parental relationship greatly influences a child's sense of personal safety and emotional security. If the relationship is faulty, or if bonding never occurs, healthy growth may not take place. In such cases, children may develop distorted perceptions about themselves and the world. This can interfere with the establishment of normal relationships in adult life.

Almost all learning in the first years of life occurs within the context of the family. Parents and adult relatives encourage children to walk and talk and, by providing a rich variety of experiences, stimulate intellectual curiosity. It is with the guidance of these interested adults that the child learns about his or her internal and external world.

The World Inside Us

Not everything a person learns is gained directly from books, teachers, or dialogue with adults. Much more subtle interactions with parents and other close acquaintances strongly affect one's emotional development. Through these interactions one develops a self-image and a sense of self-worth.

Of course, these interactions can be positive or negative. Although they may never explicitly express it, parents may send a child the message, "You are good. You are loved". This knowledge helps build a secure personality and prepares a child to deal with life's problems. Unfortunately, and often unintentionally, the message communicated is, "You are bad. You are worthless". For the child absorbing this lesson, a sense of security and value may take years to develop. Or it may never develop at all.

The World Around Us

As children learn about their inner world and thus develop emotionally, they also grow socially and learn how to interact with the surrounding world. Here, too, the family is central to learning, and it is through family relationships that the child first learns how to relate to other people.

Early in a child's life, parents' perceptions dominate. The child, having limited experience in the world, quite naturally

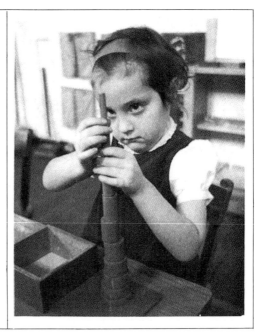

Early school days can prove crucial, for they often mark the first time a child is separated from his or her parents for an extended period of time. Here, a child concentrates on stacking cylinders in a Montessori school, named for the noted Italian doctor Maria Montessori, a pioneer in early childhood education. The Montessori approach aims at developing in children a sense of independence and responsibility.

and unconsciously accepts these perceptions as his or her own. It is through parents' eyes that the child first sees relatives and other people and learns which parts of the world are safe and friendly, or hostile and dangerous. This is the start of a person's socialization, and it continues throughout life.

As a person matures, his or her horizons and experiences broaden. At first, social interaction is limited to one-to-one relationships with parents. Soon, however, social contacts usually expand to include siblings, grandparents, aunts, uncles, and cousins. Later, the people in the immediate neighbourhood become a part of the picture. With entry into school, another social frontier is crossed. Relationships with peers develop — friendships (and enemies) may blossom. Finally, one comes into contact with the work world. And within all these relationships and environments one will always encounter varying degrees of stress.

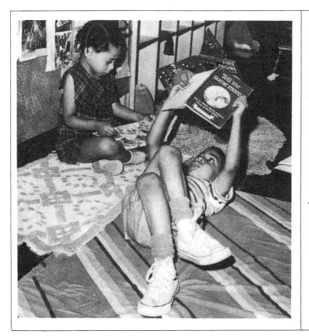

These two five-year-olds in the United States, are among the participants in a programme known as Head Start, which provides underprivileged children with an opportunity for early education. One of the goals of the programme, which grew out of Maria Montessori's work, is to instill children with a feeling of confidence and self-worth that could better prepare them for the tensions of everyday life.

The dreaded atom bomb. Although the nuclear age has provided numerous technological advantages, it has also created the nightmarish possibility of human annihilation, a major worldwide cause of stress.

CHAPTER 4

THE EMOTIONS OF STRESS

*T*here are many emotional responses to stressful situations. Stress disturbs one's equilibrium, and in an attempt to regain balance, the mind and body mobilize to adapt. The adaptive emotions experienced as a result of stress serve to warn, defend, and/or relieve. Though these emotions are often unpleasant, they are vital to the restoration of a person's normal state.

The emotions that are the result of stress fall into three basic categories: anxiety, depression, and anger. Anxiety is characterized by restlessness and is commonly described by words such as "tense", "jittery", "uptight", "nervous", and "panicky". Depression is manifested as a feeling of hopelessness; a depressed person may describe him- or herself as being sad, hopeless, down, or unhappy. Finally, anger may surface as frustration, irritability, hostility, or even violence.

Stress responses, however, do not usually occur individually. Thus, a stressful event may elicit any combination of emotions.

Anxiety

The feelings of uneasiness or apprehensiveness experienced in anticipation of a threatening situation (real or imagined) are commonly referred to as anxiety. A wide variety of situations will elicit anxiety. Competing with other people and studying for and taking tests tend to produce anxiety, as do new or unknown situations and conflicts with family and friends. Depending on many factors, including personality and mood, this response may range from vague worry to an overriding fear that something terrible — perhaps failure — is going to occur.

It is easy to understand how quarrels or other conflicts with family or friends can provoke anxiety. Such confrontations are often surrounded by a fear of physical and/or emotional injury. Though injury may rarely result, the fear is very real. Just as real is the threat to one's self-esteem: "Will this controversy show people that I am not smart enough, fast enough, attractive enough, or popular enough?" Such apprehension is a symptom of anxiety.

Anxiety is usually a warning that alerts a person to the fact that something is wrong and prepares him or her to face the anxiety-producing situation. A lack of anxiety may result in an "I-don't-care" attitude that, in fact, may increase the potential for failure. Moderate levels of anxiety, however, are beneficial. They supply motivation and added energy and increase one's ability to focus on the task at hand.

On the other hand, too much anxiety can be damaging, causing "hyped-up" and jittery feelings so intense that effective use of energies towards achieving a goal becomes impossible. Anxiety that persists for weeks or months at a time is a cause for concern. In such cases, a person may worry constantly and be unable to relax. Excessive perspiration or pounding of the heart may occur, as may difficulty in sleeping or concentrating. Although these symptoms are all associated with normal anxiety, their persistence over an extended period of time is an indication that anxiety is out of control. At that point anxiety is no longer serving as a warning, but has begun to control the individual, creating problems often unrelated to the original stressful situation.

Excessive anxiety may be caused by a number of factors. A person may just be overloaded. There may be too many important decisions to be made in too short a period of time, or too many stressful events may occur one after the other. Usually, when the crisis has passed, things return to normal. However, there are times when, regardless of external circumstances, anxiety continues. When this occurs it is important to seek parental or professional help.

Depression

Like anxiety, depression can be a protective response to certain stressors. However, unlike anxiety, depression is often experienced as a slowing down or a blunting of the effects of physical and/or emotional discomfort. Everyone has experienced depression at one time or another. Most likely, the feelings of depression followed some distressing event: the failure to achieve an important goal, rejection by a friend, the breakup of a relationship. The fundamental characteristic of depression is an unhappy mood, or "dysphoria".

Central to any discussion of depression is the concept of loss. The loss of relationships can occur through death, separation, or rejection; the loss of self-esteem through inability to live up to one's own standards or to achieve important goals; and the loss of full participation in the normal routine of life through illness, injury, or disability.

Losses such as these are frequently followed by a few hours or days of an unhappy or "down" feeling. Friends or relatives may be able to raise temporarily the sufferer's spirits,

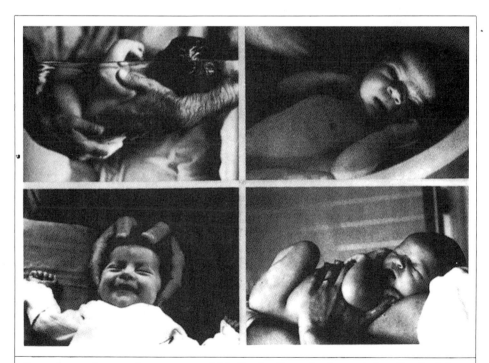

In order to lessen the trauma of birth, the French obstetrician Frederick LeBoyer developed a technique that includes the baby's immersion in warm water and that provides a more relaxed and less stressful entry into the world than do more conventional delivery procedures.

but depression usually resurfaces. Meals may be skipped and normally enjoyable situations may be avoided. Sleeping and concentration difficulties are not uncommon. Then, after dwelling on the problem for several days and perhaps talking about it with friends, the individual may gradually gain a new perspective on his or her loss. Life does not seem so hopeless — there are ways to rise above the loss, learn from what had been a depressing situation, and continue living. However, if the loss was very serious, such as the death of a parent, the healing process may take many weeks or months, if not years.

Depression can be triggered by stimuli other than loss. These can be physical, such as a biochemical change in the brain, or psychological, such as the presence of unresolved, unconscious feelings. In addition, people sometimes become very depressed for no apparent reason. Experts have identified several factors that may make an individual prone

The sense of hopelessness and loss that results from unemployment, which in the early 1980s was about 10% in most developed countries, is a depressing reality for these men, who have just been laid off.

to depression such as:

a) history of depression in close family members;
b) neglect or abuse as a child;
c) death of a parent during childhood or adolescence

Despite the seriousness of depression, it does tend to go away by itself, most often within a few days. There is some truth in the old cliché that "time heals all wounds". However, no one enjoys feeling depressed, even for a few days. Therefore, it is important to know that there are things that can be done to help get through the unavoidable low periods.

The single most important aid in overcoming depression is talking and being with other people. This is true even though people usually respond to depression by wanting to be alone. Though solitude may seem to be the most natural and easy response, it is probably the least effective way to combat depression.

Contact with others is helpful in several ways. By spending time with other people an individual learns that others care and may even have experienced similar difficulties. Friends, family, and even teachers may help the depressed individual see things in a more positive light. And

Depression and anxiety frequently follow sudden loss, evident in this picture of a mother comforting her son after the family farm was auctioned off following the death of the father.

sometimes just being with people helps. Going to see a film or taking a walk may divert one's attention from the depression and allow it to fade.

However, like anxiety, depression is sometimes more than a passing mood. When the mood persists for weeks or months, instead of just hours or days, it is called major depression. This condition generally is accompanied by several of the following additional symptoms:

difficulty in sleeping *or* excessive sleeping;
low energy, tiredness, or fatigue;
poor appetite accompanied by weight loss *or* increased appetite accompanied by weight gain;
feelings of guilt or unworthiness;
loss of interest or pleasure in usual activities;
difficulty in thinking or concentrating;
physical agitation and restlessness *or* lethargy;
thoughts of death or suicide.

Of course everyone feels down some of the time. An individual may even be troubled periodically by a few of the symptoms of major depression. However, this does not mean that he or she is suffering from major depression. Such a serious case of major depression is set apart from normal unhappiness by the inability to shake off the low mood for weeks at a time, combined with the presence of several of the symptoms listed above. People suffering from major depression should seek professional help.

Anger

Any analysis of emotional responses to stress would be incomplete without a discussion of anger. Many of the same situations that cause anxiety or depression may also trigger feelings of anger. For instance, while students may experience anxiety the night before a final exam, it is not unusual for them to also feel anger, which is usually directed at the teacher who is giving the exam.

Anger often develops when an individual perceives something obstructing his or her movement or progress, or something frustrating the attainment of a goal. Anger may also develop in response to injustice, whether one is directly or indirectly suffering from the injustice. Though it is usually directed at someone else, anger can be directed inward, in which case it usually does not last long, and either dissipates quickly or becomes transformed into feelings of anxiety or depression.

The intensity of this emotion can range from mild annoyance to seething rage. As with all emotions, anger is experienced differently by different people. Some people anger easily and often, others hardly ever and only after great provocation. What is mildly irritating to one person may be justification for a fight to another.

Anger can be released in many acceptable ways. It can be expressed outwardly and directly, such as by yelling or even threatening the offending party. Sometimes, however, it cannot be expressed directly. For example, if a student is reprimanded by a teacher, it may not be in his or her best interest to express anger directly to the teacher. What can be done to release this pent-up anger? "Talking out" the anger

A teenager, played by James Dean, grabs his passive, weak-willed father in a moment of anger in the 1956 film Rebel Without a Cause. *Family conflicts are a source of stress and alienation for many youths.*

with someone who has a sympathetic ear can help. Or one may knowingly or unknowingly direct the anger onto someone or something that cannot strike back. The dog cannot fail its master in maths.

There are other ways of expressing anger indirectly. Some people work off anger physically, such as by competing in sports. Sometimes, upon reexamination of the anger-producing situation, a person discovers that he or she had overreacted to something that would normally have been interpreted as nonthreatening. And finally — and in the long run this approach is sometimes the most productive — it is often possible to discuss the problem situation with the person who has caused the anger.

Violence is the one form of expression of anger that is rarely acceptable. People who consistently release their anger violently — hurting other people or destroying property —

A member of a street gang exposes his knife. Poverty, unemployment, poor housing, and broken homes are an understandable source of anger and frustration, which, when no alternative outlets are apparent, frequently surface as violence.

frequently have underlying psychological problems that may be traced to their childhood.

Some people, though not physically violent, may seem angry all the time. They seem hostile, always with a "chip on the shoulder". In fact, these people are probably experiencing significant feelings of depression and anxiety yet are only capable of expressing them as anger. Though these people are in great need of sympathy and understanding, their way of dealing with distress only serves to push others away and further distance them from better ways of resolving their problems.

Firming and developing muscles, building up bodily strength and lung capacity, not only improves the appearance and physical health but is also a positive way to relieve tension and anger.

At Johns Hopkins University in the United States, Dr Solomon H. Snyder and one of his assistants recently discovered the areas of the brain that are affected by narcotics. A better understanding of these areas could lead to a safe chemical treatment for heroin and cocaine addiction.

CHAPTER 5

DRUGS AND THE NERVOUS SYSTEM

*T*here are many different ways to deal with the emotional problems caused by stress. Unfortunately, many people, unwilling to take an effective but long-term approach, turn to the quick — but temporary — escape from stress provided by alcohol and drugs. While alcohol and drugs do sometimes provide temporary relief, they may also create more problems than they solve. To understand how drugs affect our minds and bodies, one must first understand the functioning of the nervous system.

How the Nervous System Works

The nervous system is a network of specialized tissues that controls the actions and reactions of the body, and enables it to adjust to changes in its environment. The nervous system, which consists of the brain, the spinal cord, and the nerves, is made up of billions of specialized cells called nerve cells. More than half of these are located in the brain.

   The nerve cells carry information from every part of the body to the brain, which then processes this data and sends information back to the relevant areas of the body. Almost all of a person's movements, sensations, thoughts, and emotions are products of these activities of the nervous system.

   To transfer information from one nerve cell to another, the body uses certain chemicals, called neurotransmitters.

These substances are released from the axon, or the end of a nerve cell, jump across the synapse, or gap, that exists between nerve cells, and bind, or attach, to the receptors of the next nerve cell. Depending on their chemical composition, neurotransmitters are excitatory (stimulating) or inhibitory (depressing). The type of neurotransmitter that is released, and the number and type of receptors to which it attaches, determine the actions and reactions of our minds and bodies.

Drugs, Alcohol, and the Nervous System

All the functions of the nervous system are dependent on the normal action of neurotransmitters. Drugs and alcohol, no matter how they are taken into the body, disrupt this action and alter the messages carried by the neurotransmitters.

Alcohol and drugs enhance, distort, or even eliminate normal information sent by the nerve cells that control the senses. This accounts for the enhanced sensations of colour and sound associated with marijuana, the hallucinations associated with LSD, and the numbing and narcotic effects of opiates and barbiturates. These drugs also act on centres of the brain where moods and emotions are regulated. Thus they can produce feelings of well-being and euphoria, as well as feelings of paranoia, fear, and depression.

Like the naturally occurring neurotransmitters in the body, the active chemicals in psychoactive drugs are broken down into inactive forms through metabolism, the process by which substances are converted into compounds easily eliminated from the body. Because of metabolism, once drug use is terminated the effects of drugs gradually wear off and the nervous system soon returns to normal functioning.

However, if the body is regularly subjected to these chemicals, permanent changes may occur. For example, in response to regular disruption of normal nerve function due to drug use, the body may reduce or completely discontinue production of a natural neurotransmitter. Furthermore, the active chemicals in abused drugs may damage certain types of bodily tissue, particularly in the brain, producing a lesion, or dead spot, that cannot recover function. Finally, the body, forced to develop abnormal methods for breaking down these foreign chemicals, may become permanently unable to carry out normal metabolism of naturally occurring neurotransmitters.

Tolerance

Tolerance is the natural or developed ability of the body to adjust to the continued or increasing use of a drug. When tolerance develops, the intensity and duration of the effects of a given drug are less profound than when the drug was first used. Tolerance is both physiological and psychological. Physiologically, the nervous system adjusts to the continued presence of the drug. Psychologically, the individual becomes accustomed to the feelings produced by the drug, thus decreasing the user's perception of the drug's effects.

The phenomenon of tolerance creates a vicious circle of drug use. As the body and mind get used to the drug, it becomes necessary to use greater quantities to reproduce the original effects. This, in turn, produces increased tolerance to the drug and a corresponding need for even higher doses. This endless cycle produces the repetitive need for the drug associated with addiction.

A major characteristic of tolerance is that it does not develop for all effects of the drug at the same time or at the same level of intake. Thus, it is possible for the positive, euphoric effects of a drug to be strong at low and infrequent doses, with relatively little sign of negative, or dysphoric, effects. However, as tolerance to the drug develops, and the dose needed to produce the desired effects increases, the probability of negative effects may grow disproportionately.

The Drug Experience

The perceived effects produced by any given drug are dependent on a great many factors. Particularly important is the quality of the drug, that is, the extent to which its chemical makeup is pure. Often drugs purchased on the street contain impurities, whose effects range from being non-existent to being dangerous or even lethal. Equally important is the physical and mental state, as well as the recent history, of the user. Finally, there is the physical and social environment in which the drug is experienced. There are many confirmed reports of "contact highs" produced by what was thought to be marijuana but was later confirmed to be only a mixture of ordinary grass, weeds, oregano, and parsley. Similarly, there have been many reports of "bummers" by individuals who found themselves in stressful situations after taking what they erroneously believed was LSD, but was in fact merely some relatively innocuous substance.

All levels of society use drinking to ease their anxiety. Alcohol's social facilitation effect — its ability to reduce social tension — is separate from its chemical effect on the body and more closely related to the familiar and comforting rituals surrounding its use.

CHAPTER 6

ALCOHOL

Alcohol is the product of the fermentation of naturally occurring sugars in fruits, grains, vegetables, and even flowers. Even when ingested in small doses it is toxic, or poisonous, to the body. Consumed in moderate to large quantities over extended periods of time, alcohol will seriously damage the heart, kidneys, stomach, and especially the liver.

Alcohol is probably the oldest man-made psychoactive, or mind-altering, substance. Despite its well-documented negative physical effects, alcohol has been almost universally used since the earliest of times to counteract unpleasant emotional states, to increase pleasure, and to promote sociability. The Psalms of the Old Testament sing of "wine that maketh glad the heart of man". And according to the ancient Roman poet Horace, "What wonders hath wine. It eases the anxious mind of its burden".

Alcohol and Social Tensions

Social gatherings are meant to be pleasureable and enjoyable, and yet frequently they are sources of anxiety. Most people at least occasionally experience feelings of inadequacy or uneasiness in a social situation. Who cannot recall that uncomfortable moment at a party, when, after being introduced to a new person, no particularly amusing or interesting conversation piece came to mind?

In these situations alcohol is used to ease social tension, which it does in several ways. The alcoholic drink, which is usually chilled, refreshes a palate dry from anxiety. Rather than being forced to stand awkwardly with hands in pockets or to shift restlessly from foot to foot, the drinker is also provided with something to do. And, since the majority of adults do drink, participation in drinking customs emphasizes a common link between fellow socializers. Thus these functions of alcohol ease tension and increase the possibility of enjoying oneself.

This characteristic of alcohol to ease social tension is called the social facilitation effect of alcohol. It is separate from the chemical effect of alcohol, and is felt even *before* the alcohol is ingested. In many ways, the social context in which one drinks may even determine alcohol's overall effects on the body.

Because of the alcohol facilitation effect, the anxiety experienced in a social situation can be reduced merely by participating in the act of drinking and never consuming any alochol. For example, problem drinkers who have given up alcohol often report that they feel left out at parties. However, many of these people have discovered that by joining the group but drinking only nonalcoholic beverages, they can enjoy the positive effects of drinking without suffering the negative physical consequences.

People who have come to rely on 'props' such as alcohol to relieve tension and anxiety are at a disadvantage when faced with a tense situation — such as sitting exams — where alcohol could impair their ability and a "couple of quick ones" could lead to failure.

Pharmacologic Effects of Alcohol

It would be inaccurate to claim that the major mood-altering effects of alcohol are due only to the drinking environment. Clearly, if this were true, alcohol would not be used as widely as it is. In fact, alcohol has a number of pharmacological properties that cause it to alter sensations, feelings, and abilities, regardless of the social setting.

Virtually all drugs have varied and increasingly stronger effects as they are used over a period of time and in greater doses. This is especially true for alcohol.

The dual nature of alcohol's effects has been known since alcohol was first used. Initially, alcohol is a stimulant and releaser of energy, but after time, and at larger doses, it acts as a strong depressant. One chemist, noting these contradictory characteristics, has called alcohol a "great deceiver".

Many studies have focused on alcohol's mood-changing qualities. The data are very clear. Using low doses of alcohol for short periods appears to liven spirits and produce greater happiness in normal people. Low doses also appear to reduce feelings of anxiety and depression in both normal and

At social gatherings, alcohol can relax people not only by producing its physiological effects, but by providing a context for familiar rituals.

depressed people. High doses of alcohol, or moderate doses over longer periods, do not have mood-elevating effects on either of these groups of people. On the contrary, these higher doses can cause increased anxiety and depression in both normal and depressed people. Among alcoholics, the higher doses produce variable effects, none of them clearly positive.

Despite these findings, most people who use alcohol tend to remember only the light-use, low-dose, positive effects. They may recall how small amounts of alcohol helped lift their mood and relieve tension when a personal problem had made them depressed, frustrated, or insecure. Even heavy drinkers and alcoholics usually believe that using alcohol will raise their mood, decrease their anxiety, and improve their sleep.

These erroneous impressions have also been studied. Apparently, people in general, and heavy drinkers in particular, selectively remember the initial, low-dose, pleasant effects of alcohol and are generally less able to recall the later, high-dose, unpleasant effects. This phenomenon may be due to memory impairment caused by higher doses of alcohol, and is probably one of the reasons why heavy drinkers continue to abuse alcohol despite its adverse effects.

Tolerance

If alcohol is used frequently the body will develop a tolerance to it, and its positive effects against feelings of loneliness, anxiety, depression, and insecurity will diminish. On the other hand, alcohol's negative effects on mood, energy level, and sleep and its tendency to heighten feelings of anxiety will become more profound. Not only will alcohol become ineffective as a means of dealing with stress, it will actually produce or magnify the very symptoms of anxiety and depression the drinker was originally trying to escape.

Alcohol Abuse

Alcohol's positive effects occur only at low doses and generally only in appropriate social surroundings, such as at parties, other social events, and gatherings with fellow workers. This form of use is generally considered appropriate and responsible. In these situations, the positive effects of alcohol can be enjoyed and the negative effects minimized.

Most people initially use alcohol to enjoy the positive feelings associated with social drinking. However, many people later try to use alcohol as a tool to overcome emotional problems. Millions of people — including teenagers — throughout the world have suffered from alcohol abuse, which has led to addiction, physical disease, and/or psychological illness. Alcohol should never be thought of as a medicine or used as an escape from problems.

Betty Ford, wife of a former American president, recovered from a dependency on pills and alcohol and discussed her problems frankly and publicly. After her recovery, Mrs Ford opened the Betty Ford Centre for Chemical Dependency, a rehabilitation centre in southern California.

The Chinese characters for cannabis, the psychoactive marijuana plant. Use of marijuana goes back almost 5,000 years, to a time when the Chinese referred to the drug as the "liberator of sin".

CHAPTER 7

MARIJUANA

Marijuana, the common name for *Cannabis sativa* or *Cannabis indica,* is a plant that grows in virtually all climates and countries of the world. Cannabis contains hundreds of unique chemicals known as cannabinoids. Although at least 60 of these have intoxicating effects, the primary psychoactive component is Delta-9-THC, most often referred to as THC. Though THC can be ingested by smoking the plant's resins or by eating or smoking the dried leaves, most frequently the leaves are smoked in cigarette-like "joints". Inhaling the smoke brings both inactive agents, such as tars, carbon monoxide, and other particles, and psychoactive ingredients into the lungs, from which they are absorbed into the blood stream.

The "high" produced by marijuana is due to the actions of the cannabinoids on nerve receptors in the brain. Characteristic effects include the enhancement of sight, sound, and taste, a general feeling of relaxation, and the loss of tension. Because of these positive effects, marijuana is often used to assist relaxation and to enhance the enjoyment of already pleasurable activities, such as dancing, listening to music, or attending concerts. In addition, because of its sensory-stimulating effects, the drug is used by some individuals to heighten interest during repetitive or boring tasks.

As with other drugs, marijuana's effects depend on a variety of factors. Naturally, the size of the dose is very important: the larger the dose, the greater the effect. The environment in which marijuana is used also influences the nature and extent of its effects. Marijuana ingested in a relaxed, enjoyable atmosphere will often evoke pleasurable feelings. However, marijuana used in surroundings filled with hostility, tension, or fear will often only magnify these unpleasant emotions in the user.

Perhaps the most important factor in determining marijuana's effects is the previous drug history of the individual user. Frequent users develop tolerance, and therefore require more of the drug to produce the same intensity of effects previously experienced with lower doses. The phenomenon of marijuana tolerance has another, more disturbing, feature: the larger doses ingested by tolerant heavy users often produce frightening and undesired effects, experiences of which are sometimes called "bummers".

Who Uses Marijuana and Why?

Marijuana is the most commonly used illegal drug in the Western world. Use varies, however, between countries. For example in the United Kingdom about 30% of young people have tried it, in the United States this figure increases to 50%.

In countries where marijuana is more socially acceptable national surveys have not been able to find any significant demographic, personality, or other background characteristics associated with marijuana users. That is, people who have tried marijuana are not particularly different from those who have not tried it. Furthermore, there is no longer the social stigma attached to those who have tried it.

There are, however, profound differences between the casual or one-time user and the regular user. These differences range from performance in school or work to overall satisfaction with life. In general, those who become regular users (defined as three or more times a week) begin using the drug earlier than those who become casual users (once a week or less). More than 30% of regular users reported that they started use before reaching the age of twelve. Regular users are also seven times more likely than casual users to be using additional illicit drugs, such as speed and/or barbiturates. Among senior school pupils, those who report regular use of marijuana have significantly poorer grades and are only half as likely to enter college or pursue other further education as their casual or non-using peers. Finally, regular marijuana users who have left school have significantly lower incomes and report being less satisfied with their work than working people of the same age who do not use marijuana regularly, or, indeed, have never used it at all.

It is important to ask whether marijuana serves the same function for the regular, daily user and the casual, infrequent user. Responding to a national survey in the United States, virtually all marijuana users, casual and regular, gave the same reasons for starting to smoke: "to feel good or get high" (95%), "to have a good time with my friends" (79%), and "because my friends urged me" (61%).

When casual users were asked about their current reasons for marijuana use, the first two answers — "to feel good" and "to have a good time" — still prevailed overwhelmingly. In contrast, while regular marijuana users also continued to cite these two reasons, large numbers additionally responded, "to get away from my problems" (37%) or "to help me get through the day" (29%). Using

Medical use of marijuana is approved in some countries. John Nash, a lung cancer victim, was the first court-approved marijuana smoker in Texas, USA. Legal arrangements were made for him to use the drug, which is helpful in relieving the nausea caused by chemotherapy, thereby decreasing the anxiety associated with the treatment.

marijuana as a means of escaping or coping with problems thus strongly distinguishes the regular daily user of marijuana from the casual user.

From these results one may be tempted to conclude that regular marijuana users simply have more frustrations and daily problems than casual users, and that marijuana, with its ability to intensify sensations, interest, and pleasure, is effective in relieving these pressures. However, the same survey asked senior school pupils who were formerly daily users of marijuana why they stopped heavy use. The answers would seem to eliminate marijuana as an effective, long-term stress reliever. Of those questioned, 56% responded that they "weren't getting high anymore", 38% said they were "worried about physical effects", and 41% said they were "concerned about psychological changes", specifically loss of energy and motivation. Given these results, it is doubtful that marijuana is useful in alleviating the problems of boredom, depression, and tension commonly experienced by all people, and often especially by adolescents.

Those who continue to use the drug infrequently tend to report that even years later marijuana continues to produce the same positive effects it did during the first experience. In contrast, however, those individuals who use marijuana regularly to ease anxiety, tension, and depression became heavy users, though they generally experience a gradual decrease in the drug's effectiveness. For example, the shy student who finds that his or her initial nervousness at a party is relieved by marijuana may smoke *prior* to attending the next party; later, that student may even smoke prior to giving an oral report in class. However, though this strategy for relieving stress may work for a while, the fact that it does not work over the long term is evidenced by numerous studies. In fact, the daily users grow even more bored, have poorer and more incomplete educations, and are generally more dissatisfied with life than their nonsmoking peers.

That marijuana is at least partially responsible for the unsatisfying lives frequently reported by regular users is supported by the assertions of many former heavy users. They often state they quit marijuana use because, instead of heightening sensation and increasing enjoyment, the daily, heavy use of the drug was instead decreasing their energy and enthusiasm. Ironically, although they were smoking more, they were enjoying the effects less. Thus, what seems at first like a good strategy for handling stress ultimately becomes ineffective and self-destructive.

Effects of Long-Term Use

In 1983 the National Academy of Sciences in the United States issued a comprehensive report on the positive and negative aspects of marijuana entitled *Marijuana and Health*. According to this report, there are many long-term physical effects of marijuana use, but of particular interest here is the ironic fact that chronic marijuana use affects the heart and lungs in ways very similar to prolonged stress! The available data indicate that, just like physical and emotional stress,

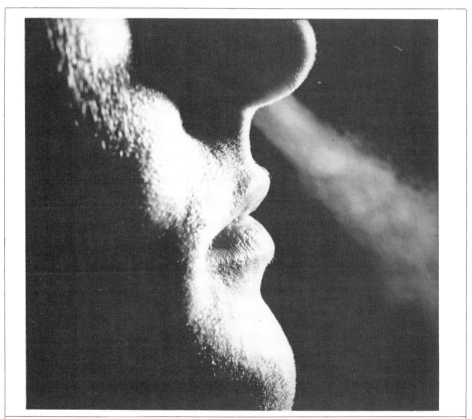

The majority of people who use marijuana inhale it mixed with burning tobacco. Chronic long-term use can cause serious psychological problems and further, can greatly increase the stress which perhaps originated its use.

marijuana use increases the work of the heart by raising the heart rate and increasing blood pressure. Thus, the protracted use of the drug to release stress and tension actually has the opposite effect, at least on the heart and lungs.

The long-term effects of marijuana on mood and behaviour are even more intriguing. First-time users almost universally report positive effects from the drug. However, 33% of regular users report that while intoxicated they sometimes experience such symptoms as acute panic, paranoia, hallucinations, and unpleasant perceptual distortions. Studies also show that "stable, well-adjusted, moderate users" report similar negative experiences from marijuana use.

The unpleasant emotional effects experienced by these moderate users may have resulted from stressful, threatening factors in the surroundings in which the marijuana was used. However, it is also likely that the bad experiences may have been the result of the increased dosage of the drug required by chronic marijuana users to obtain the desired high. This is a graphic illustration of what was mentioned earlier: tolerance to many of the pleasant effects of marijuana develops after prolonged use, and as increased amounts of the drug are used to duplicate the pleasant effects previously experienced, the risk of unpleasant effects increases.

There are numerous other significant emotional consequences associated with the chronic, long-term use of marijuana. Of these, one of the most serious is *acute brain syndrome,* a condition marked by perceptual distortions; sleep and memory problems; disorientation with regard to time and place; and the inability to concentrate or sustain attention to important stimuli in the environment. Acute brain syndrome requires hospital treatment and, fortunately, the symptoms seem to diminish and eventually disappear one or two months after discontinuation of marijuana use.

Amotivational syndrome is a less severe but more common condition seen in chronic marijuana users. It is characterized by symptoms such as apathy, loss of effectiveness, loss of ambition, and diminished ability to carry out plans. Amotivational syndrome occurs with varying degrees of severity in 30 to 60% of persons who have smoked marijuana regularly over a five-year period. Although amotivational syndrome is also seen in people who do not use drugs, there is clear evidence linking it to marijuana use.

Summary

The available data offer a conclusion on the use of marijuana to alleviate stress, provide stimulation, and intensify pleasure: marijuana may be temporarily effective for these purposes under certain conditions, but only when use is infrequent. Regular use reduces the drug's ability to produce favourable effects and, ironically, leads to increased stress on the heart and lungs, increased apathy and boredom, and increased risk of anxiety and panic attacks. Thus, what may appear to be a simple solution to the common problems of boredom, anxiety and depression may readily come to exaggerate the initial problems and produce new ones as well.

The business of marijuana supply is a multimillion dollar industry. People go to great lengths to protect their contraband.

A late 1890s advertisement for Coca-Cola. The claim that the beverage could relieve exhaustion has some basis. Until the 1920s coke contained a small amount of the stimulant cocaine and since has contained the less powerful stimulant caffeine.

CHAPTER 8

STIMULANTS

Stimulant drugs include amphetamine, cocaine, caffeine, and other preparations such as methylphenidate (Ritalin). These drugs have a general stimulating effect on the brain and body, and thus produce feelings of power, energy, and euphoria as well as heightened sensitivity to stimuli. Stimulant drugs may be taken in several forms. For example, most users of cocaine inhale, or "snort", the drug in white powder form. Amphetamine users may ingest the large dark pills known as "black beauties" or inject cooked or liquid forms of methamphetamine, or "speed".

Unlike many of the other commonly abused drugs, stimulants such as amphetamine and methylphenidate are prescribed by doctors for medical problems. For many years these drugs have been used in the treatment of hyperactive children. These children have great difficulty attending to any fixed task and are often hyperactive and uncontrollable, especially in school. Although it may seem odd that a stimulant is used to reduce activity, in small doses these drugs have an action on the brain that improves attention and focuses energy, thereby reducing random activity.

It is this ability to increase attention, energy, and feelings of power and ability that has attracted attention to the stimulants during the past century. Sigmund Freud, the great physician and founder of psychoanalysis, studied and used cocaine for several years. In his early works written in the late 19th century he praised the stimulant action of the drug as a remedy for exhaustion and advocated its use to stimulate "clarity of thinking". At one point he recommended cocaine to a friend for easing pain; the friend rapidly became dependent on the drug, using as much as 1 gram a day (0.2 gm of cocaine being an average daily dose for today's user). Freud's description of his friend's "delirium" — extreme confusion and problems with attention — during heavy cocaine use is probably the first recorded case of cocaine psychosis. Freud dropped his earlier advocacy of cocaine use, stopped his personal use, and even published warnings about the drug. Despite this, many medical historians have accused Freud of unleashing the "third scourge of humanity", the other two being alcohol and opiates (heroin and morphine).

Who Uses Stimulants and Why?

Many people begin to use stimulants because they find that small doses make them feel stronger and more energetic, and

Sigmund Freud (1856 – 1939), the Austrian physician and father of psychoanalysis. Though in his early writing, most notably the book Über Coca, *Freud advocated the therapeutic use of cocaine, subsequent observations of the drug's dangers led him to publish warnings against its use. In fact, until recently these works contained the most definitive description of cocaine's psychological and physiological effects.*

at the same time calmer and more confident. Obviously, these effects have much appeal, particularly to students who "cram" for examinations, people who must work long hours or at more than one job, and athletes who wish to improve performance.

The stimulants' positive effects are even more attractive to people who are unable to concentrate, are normally unsure of themselves in performance situations, or who are suffering from mild symptoms of depression or low self-esteem. For people with these and similar problems, using stimulants makes them feel considerably more confident. At higher doses, these drugs produce sensory excitation and feelings of euphoria.

Development of Dependence

Negative reactions due to the use of stimulants generally develop in the same fashion as with other drugs. At first the user finds the drug useful in an ever-widening range of stressful situations and increases frequency of use. As frequency of use increases, the process of tolerance reduces the pleasurable effects of the drug at lower dosage levels. To duplicate the original positive effects, the individual increases the dosage, and the drug's unwanted side effects occur more frequently and become stronger. In fact, with the possible exception of alcohol, there is no class of drugs so dangerous.

Perhaps the most widespread and well-known side effect associated with the use of stimulants is the depression that occurs when regular drug use is discontinued. It is ironic that these drugs, which when taken regularly can be so effective in reducing depression, when discontinued produce such dramatic increases in that very same depressive condition. Perhaps most unfortunate is the fact that the most effective means of reversing the depressive state is through readministration of the drug. Thus begins the vicious circle of events that ends in drug dependence.

This withdrawal reaction — an increase in depressive symptoms — can occur even at low doses of the drug if the drug has been used regularly. Withdrawal symptoms include fatigue, lowered energy level, bodily pain, sleep problems, and a generalized deepening of the depressed state. These symptoms can last for as long as a week after a six-month period of regular use, and as long as a month following longer periods of use.

Stimulant Psychosis

Even more serious than the common symptom of post-use depression is the well-documented phenomenon known as stimulant psychosis. The major characteristic of stimulant psychosis is paranoia. As used here, this word goes far beyond its popular meaning of generalized suspiciousness or even unreasonable fear.

The paranoia associated with stimulant psychosis can be more accurately described as terror born of wild, irrational fears about people and places in the environment. To a person experiencing stimulant psychosis, a group of people waiting for a bus on a street corner may be seen with absolute certainty as a gang of terrorists waiting to attack. It is not an overstatement, nor is it meant as a scare tactic, to stress that stimulant psychosis can occur in almost any user of stimulant drugs under certain dosage conditions and in certain situations.

Toxic psychosis, as this condition is also called, is caused by the action of the stimulant drug on the nervous system. It usually occurs in individuals who have used abnormally high doses of a stimulant, or in individuals who, although not exceeding normal dosages, have used the drug with much greater frequency than usual — so-called binge use. (Psychotic behaviour is also associated with heavy use of other classes of drugs, such as some of the tranquillizers [Valium, Ativan], and with hallucinogenic drugs such as LSD, PCP, peyote, and mescaline.)

Psychotic episodes in response to heavy stimulant use are not confined to those few individuals with possible preexisting psychiatric problems or psychoses. Extensive studies have shown that the behaviour produced by high doses of amphetamines or cocaine in volunteers with no prior history of stimulant use is virtually identical to the behaviour seen in patients suffering from acute schizophrenia.

Even in less severe instances, episodes of stimulant psychosis are often accompanied by violence and injury. Perhaps most troubling, however, is the possibility raised by the results of the psychological testing of individuals who have had successive periods of heavy stimulant use. These tests indicate that in some cases the short-term, toxic states are not fully reversible. That is, some heavy, long-term users of stimulant drugs may never fully return to normal after an episode of stimulant psychosis.

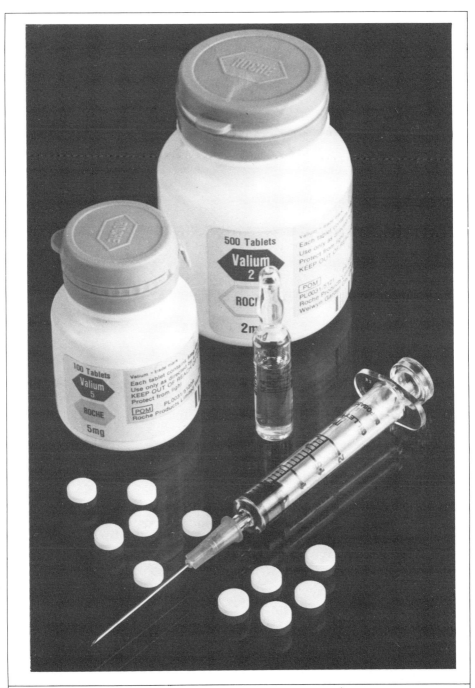

People who inadvertently become addicted to legally prescribed tranquillizers, such as Valium, find their behaviour and mood frighteningly altered when they suddenly stop taking it. Drug-induced paranoia, panic attacks and loss of motor control are just some of the withdrawal symptoms exhibited.

71

Clubs of any type, bringing together like-minded people to pursue a mutual hobby, could probably promote their activities as a therapeutic means to relieve daily stress.

CHAPTER 9

ARE DRUGS USEFUL FOR HANDLING STRESS?

Stress is a natural consequence of living and can be either negative (distress) or positive (eustress). This book has concentrated generally on negative stress, and particularly on some of the emotional states that accompany it: anxiety, depression, and anger.

Everyone experiences these emotions in varying degrees and at various times, and it is important to develop strategies and skills to deal with them. One popular coping strategy, especially among people during their school years, is the use of street drugs and alcohol. The issue of whether or not drugs help one handle stress would be simple if it were possible to claim that alcohol and street drugs are not at all effective in dealing with the unpleasant emotions of stress. However, drugs do exert a powerful influence over negative emotional states, and thus can often provide quick relief from many of life's pressures. Less readily apparent, but equally true and perhaps more important, is that this relief is only temporary and carries with it some terrible risks.

Regular use of drugs at low-dosage levels leads to tolerance. Higher doses become necessary to produce the desired effects, but with the high doses comes the increased likelihood of unwanted side effects. In addition, chronic use at higher-dosage levels may produce more serious — and perhaps irreversible — physical and emotional problems.

Given these facts, why has drug use become such a popular way to handle stress-related problems?

It would seem that the major attraction of drug use as a strategy for handling stress lies in the fact that it is quick and easy. However, there are many other ways of handling stress, such as practicing a form of meditation or using biofeedback (both of which can provide profound relaxation as well as a sense of expanded consciousness and awareness), developing new interests, and performing vigorous physical exercise. These approaches require more energy, time, and patience than popping a pill or passing around a "joint". Indeed, some of these slower methods may even involve stress in their development. But their advantage is that they are safe and effective, not just for a few hours, but for a lifetime. Development of long-term strategies and skills for dealing with stress gives confidence and helps an individual achieve independence.

Four monks pass a statue of a recumbent Buddha in Japan. The historical Buddha reportedly became enlightened while meditating, a practice used today by many people to overcome anxiety and stress.

Further Reading

Mathews, Andrew. *Coping with Anxiety*. London: St George's Hospital, 1980.

Selye, Hans. *The Stress of Life*. New York: McGraw Hill, 1976.

Sharpe, Robert and Lewis, David. *Anxiety Antidote*. Stresswatch Publication, 3 Lauder Road, Edinburgh, Scotland.

Sutherland, F.N. *Teach Yourself to Relax*. London: English University Press, 1976.

Varma, V.P. *Stresses in Children*. New York: Crane, Russak, 1973.

Weeks, Claire. *Self-Help for Your Nerves*. London: Angus & Robertson, 1962.

Weeks, Claire. *Peace from Nervous Suffering*. London: Angus & Robertson, 1972.

Some Useful Addresses

In the United Kingdom

Manic Depression Fellowship
51 Sheen Road, Richmond, Surrey TW9 1YG.

Mental Health Foundation
8 Hallam Street, London W1N 6DY.

MIND
22 Harley Street, London W1N 2ED.

Northern Ireland Association for Mental Health
84 University Street, Belfast B17 3JR.

Scottish Association for Mental Health
40 Shandwick Place, Edinburgh EH2 4RT.

In Australia

Association of Relatives and Friends of the Mentally Ill
311 Hay Street, Subiaco, Western Australia 6008.

Australian National Association for Mental Health
1 Cookson Street, Campberwell, Victoria, Australia 3124.

In New Zealand

The Foundation
PO Box 5367, Wellesley, Auckland.

Mental Health Foundation of New Zealand
PO Box 37483, Parnell, Auckland.

In South Africa

Lifeline Personal Counselling Service
56 Roland Street, Cape Town 8001.

Glossary

acute brain syndrome   a condition resulting from chronic, long-term use of marijuana and characterized by perceptual distortions; sleep and memory problems; disorientation with regard to time and place; and an inability to concentrate on important stimuli in the environment

addiction   a condition caused by repeated drug use, characterized by a compulsive urge to continue using the drug, a tendency to increase the dosage, and physiological and/or psychological dependence

amotivational syndrome   a condition associated with chronic marijuana users and characterized by apathy, loss of ambition and effectiveness, and diminished ability to carry out plans

amphetamine   a drug that stimulates the nervous system; generally used as a mood elevator, energizer, antidepressant, and appetite depressant

anxiety   an emotional state caused by uncertainty, apprehension, fear, and/or dread that produces such symptoms as sweating, agitation, and increased blood pressure and heart rate

axon   the part of a neuron along which the nerve impulse travels away from the cell body

barbiturate   a drug that causes depression of the central nervous system; generally used to reduce anxiety or to induce euphoria

caffeine   trimethylxanthine; a central nervous system stimulant found in coffee, tea, cocoa, various soft drinks, and often in combination with other drugs to enhance their effects

cocaine   the primary psychoactive ingredient in the coca plant and a behavioural stimulant

dendrite   the hairlike structure which protrudes from the neural cell body on which receptor sites are located

depression   a sometimes overwhelming emotional state characterized by feelings of inadequacy and hopelessness and accompanied by a decrease in physical and psychological activity

dysphoria   the fundamental characteristic of depression; opposite to euphoria

drug   any substance — plant, powder, solid, fluid, or gas

— that when ingested, injected, sniffed, inhaled, or absorbed from the skin affects bodily functions

euphoria a mental high characterized by a sense of well-being

eustress positive stress which is pleasant or curative and serves as a stimulus to action

fermentation a chemical process by which yeast consumes sugars, such as those in fruits, and produces effervescence and alcohol

hallucination a sensory impression that has no basis in external stimulation

heroin a semisynthetic opiate produced by a chemical modification of morphine

lesion an abnormal and usually permanent change in the structure of a bodily organ due to injury or disease; specifically, a dead spot in the brain sometimes caused by drugs such as alcohol

LSD lysergic acid diethylamide; a hallucinogen derived from a fungus that grows on rye or from morning-glory seeds

marijuana the leaves, flowers, buds, and/or branches of the hemp plant *Cannabis sativa* or *Cannabis indica* that contain cannabinoids, a group of intoxicating drugs

mescaline a hallucinogenic drug found in certain cacti, chemically similar to amphetamine

metabolism the chemical changes in the living cell by which energy is provided for the vital processes and activities and by which new material is assimilated to repair cell structures; or, the process that uses enzymes to convert one substance into compounds that can be easily eliminated from the body

methamphetamine a popular form of amphetamine frequently ingested intravenously

methylphenidate a drug mainly used to treat hyperactive children; commonly known by its trade name, Ritalin

morphine the principal psychoactive ingredient of opium which produces sleep or a state of stupor; the standard against which all morphine-like drugs are compared

neurotransmitter a chemical, such as ACh, that travels from the axon of one neuron, across the synaptic gap, and to the receptor site on the dendrite of an adjacent neuron, thus allowing communication between neural cells

opiates compounds from the milky juice of the poppy plant *Papaver somniferum,* including opium, morphine, codeine, and their derivatives, such as heroin

paranoia a mental condition characterized by extreme suspiciousness, fear, delusions, and in extreme cases hallucinations

PCP phencyclidine; a drug first used as an anaesthetic but later discontinued because of its adverse side effects; today abused for its stimulant, depressant, and/or hallucinogenic effects

peyote a cactus that contains mescaline, a hallucinogenic drug, and is used legally by certain American Indians for religious and medical purposes

physical dependence an adaptation of the body to the presence of a drug such that its absence produces withdrawal symptoms

psychological dependence a condition in which the drug user craves a drug to maintain a sense of well-being and feels discomfort when deprived of it

psychotherapy a treatment of mental or emotional disorders or maladjustments using psychological methods

psychoactive altering mood and/or behaviour

receptor site a specialized area located on a dendrite which, when bound by a sufficient number of neurotransmitter molecules, produces an electrical charge

schizophrenia a chronic psychotic disorder with predominant symptoms such as paranoia, delusions, and hallucinations

stimulant any drug that increases behavioural activity

stimulant psychosis toxic psychosis; a condition caused by the action of a high dose of a stimulant on the nervous system, characterized by extreme paranoia, and often accompanied by violence and injury; this condition is sometimes irreversible

stress the nonspecific response of the body to any intellectual, emotional, and/or physical demand

stressor any condition that causes stress

synapse the gap between the axon and dendrite of two adjacent neurons in which neurotransmitters travel

THC tetra-hydrocannabinol; the psychoactive ingredient in marijuana

tolerance a decrease of susceptibility to the effects of a drug due to its continued administration, resulting in the

user's need to increase the drug dosage in order to
achieve the effects experienced previously

toxin   any substance that causes temporary or permanent
damage to cells or organ systems of the body

tranquillizer   a drug that has calming, relaxing effects

withdrawal   the physiological and psychological effects
of discontinued usage of a drug

Index

Tom McLellan, Ph.D., received his degree in psychology from Bryn Mawr College. He is currently the director of clinical research at the Philadelphia Hospital and associate professor of psychiatry at the University of Pennsylvania.

Alicia Bragg, M.A., received her degree in counseling from Rhode Island College. Before joining the research staff at the Philadelphia V.A. Hospital, Ms. Bragg counseled adolescents with alcohol and drug problems at Berks Youth Counseling Center in Reading, Pennsylvania.

John Cacciola, M.A., was educated at Vassar College, Yale University, and Temple University, where he received his degree in psychology. He is an expert in the diagnosis and treatment of psychiatric problems among substance abusers.

Solomon H. Snyder, M.D., is Distinguished Service Professor of Neuroscience, Pharmacology and Psychiatry at The Johns Hopkins University School of Medicine. He has served as president of the Society for Neuroscience and in 1978 received the Albert Laster Award in Medical Research. He has authored *Uses of Marijuana, Madness and the Brain, The Troubled Mind, Biological Aspects of Mental Disorder,* and edited *Perspective in Neuropharmacology: A Tribute to Julius Axelrod,* Professor Snyder was a research associate with Dr Axelrod at the National Institutes of Health.

Malcolm Lader; D.Sc., Ph.D., M.D., F.R.C. Psych. is Professor of Clinical Psychopharmacology at the Institute of Psychiatry, University of London, and Honorary Consultant to the Bethlem Royal and Maudsley Hospitals. He is a member of the External Scientific Staff of the Medical Research Council. He has researched extensively into the actions of drugs used to treat psychiatric illnesses and symptoms, in particular the tranquillizers. He has written several books and over 3200 scientific articles. Professor Lader is a member of several governmental advisory committees concerned with drugs.

Malcolm S. Bruce, M.R.C. Psych., is currently undertaking research into the effects of caffeine at the Institute of Psychiatry, London. His initial training in medicine was in Scotland. This was followed by specialization in psychiatry at St Thomas' Hospital, London. Since 1985 he has been in his present post as a Ph.D. student.